You Can Never Outgrow I Am

Also:

Before Abraham, Was I Am

I Am In You

I Am *the* Cause

I Am *the* Lord

Neville Goddard

You Can Never Outgrow I Am

A man can never outgrow or lose the God he knows in a first person, present tense experience. And when he finds this God he tells his brothers, saying: "If I had not come and spoken to you, you would have no sin, but now you have no excuse for your sins." God reveals himself to man as his eternal contemporary, saying: "Unless you believe that I am he, you will die in your sins," but man finds it almost impossible to keep the tense. He thinks of God in the third person, addresses him in the second person, but can only know God in a first person, present tense experience. Just imagine – no one can sin until God reveals himself to the individual in a first person, present tense experience. Only then can man have no excuse for his sin. And when one who finds God tells his brothers, he receives no greater reception than the first one did, because they see him as a man of flesh and blood, and cannot see this invisible being who says: "I came down from heaven." Man is looking for Christ to come from without, but his revelation is whispered from within.

"I tell you: I have been crucified with Christ. It is not I who lives, but Christ who lives in me. And the life I now live in the flesh I live by faith in the Son of God, who loved me and gave himself for me." In that act he, whose name is I AM, became me. And if I do not believe that my I amness is he, I will die in my sin.

When asked to identify his Father, he said: "If you knew me, you would not ask, for no man can know me without knowing God, for he and I are one." This is not a physical man speaking to another, but self speaking to self. What child is not aware that he (or she) is? And to be aware is to say, "I am," the name God revealed to Moses on the mountaintop. All things are possible to God, but man has difficulty keeping the tense. He speaks of God in third person, prays to God in the second person, but can only know God in first person, present tense, for "I am the Lord, thy God and besides me there is no other God." In the 50th Psalm these words

3

are put into the mouth of David: "Against thee and against thee only have I sinned." Only I, who must know myself in a first person present tense experience, have sinned and I have only sinned against myself!

Do you believe that Jesus Christ is in you as your very self? Are you willing to test yourself? Let me tell you of one lady who did. Many years ago while living in a rooming house in Brooklyn, with very little money, this lady started each day with these words: "I am a very wealthy woman. I have $50,000 in cash." Every Sunday morning she would go to the corner and buy a Sunday Times for her neighbor, Miss Mead, who was a little old lady living frugally and rarely left the house. Within a year after this lady began starting her day claiming her wealth, Miss Mead died, leaving her $50,000 in cash, plus jewelry valued in excess of $30,000. She received an estate of over $100,000 by keeping God in the present tense.

My friend has now found him and I want all who hear me to find him, for when you find this God you will never outgrow – and therefore never lose – him, for you can never grow outside of self. You may believe in astrology, and outgrowing that belief you may then believe in tea leaves. Outgrowing that, you will find something else to believe in as you grow and outgrow, grow and outgrow; but you cannot outgrow the God you find in the first person, present tense, for when you find him to be your I amness, you have found the only God. One day everyone will find him and join their brothers who, already awakened, are in eternity contemplating this world of death, watching for the little stir of life.

I have been sent to tell you these things, for if I had not come and spoken to you, you would have no sin. You could not miss the mark because you did not have any, but now you have no excuse for missing it. I have revealed God to you in first person saying: "He who sees me sees him who sent me." I was sent by my Father, he whom you call God, only I know my Father and you know not your God, for I know that I and my Father are one.

In the 1st chapter of Colossians, Paul tells us: "The gospel which you have heard has been preached to every creature under heaven," and in the 3rd chapter of Galatians he states: "The

4

scripture, foreseeing that all would be saved through faith, preached the gospel beforehand to Abraham, saying, "In you shall all the nations be blessed." In the state of faith called Abraham we heard the story and then went astray. Falling asleep, we forgot our true identity and worshiped idols. Speaking of God in the third person, and to him in the second person, we have forgotten the God who gave us birth. Yet I tell you: God is eternally contemporary for he is our awareness of being.

Now, without faith it is impossible to please God, and faith does work on this level. Everything you possess was brought into being through faith, and the glory of faith lies in its power to link us to the heavenly realm. Having heard salvation's story, can you have faith in this divine vision (which is the gospel) in the time of trouble? No matter what happens to you, can you center yourself upon the vision? Can you believe that, housed within you as your I amness, is the only creative power in the world? I hope so, because your faith in God is measured by your confidence in yourself.

When you imagine a state, do you believe that the scene has the power to externalize itself? Or do you feel you must pray to a being on the outside for help? I tell you: there is no being on the outside. The creative power of the world is housed within you now. Sit down and imagine a state of confidence that it must externalize itself. Believe that because all things are possible to imagine, the state you have imagined must become an external fact.

I have tried this time and time again, and it has always proved itself in performance. Now I share this knowledge with everyone who will listen. How many believe my words and put them into practice I do not know. I only know that man finds it hard to keep the tense. Religious leaders speak of God in the third person as if he were on the outside, yet I tell you he comes from within. When Moses heard the words: "I AM has sent me unto you," it seemed to come from without, yet it was whispered from within.

There is no evidence of an historical Jesus Christ. We have the essence of Christ, but not an historical one. The being within me that is speaking, is the Christ, but that which is talking to you is only a garment. Everyone knows its background. Its parents are known, its physical brothers and its limitations; yet the being wearing this garment of flesh came out from God who is my

Father, for I am from above. The body I wear is from below. I am in the world but not of it, for the being who awoke within me is the one speaking to you now. It is not the same being who entertains guests in our home or enjoys dining in a good restaurant, for this being is not in any way a part of this world. This is the being in you that I am trying to reach tonight, trying to stir and awaken to return to the one grand I AM.

Believe me when I tell you the only purpose in life is to discover who you are. Against thee, O Lord, and thee only have I sinned. Addressing him in the second person as "against thee," he realizes the Lord is within him; that he is the "I" of man who inspired the prophets to write what they did. Having conceived the play and coming out from the Father to play it, "I" must fulfill what I foretold I would do, and I will.

Christianity is based upon the affirmation that a certain series of supernatural events happened in which God revealed himself in action for the salvation of man. I have experienced every one of these events. As each event took place I recorded the date in my bible, even to a simple little one like: "What you must do, do quickly." Against that statement I marked the date of October 10, 1966, for I had been preaching to a group of twelve men, all seated on the floor, when one man jumped up and departed quickly. Then a man dressed in costly robes entered, approached me and unveiled my arm revealing the arm of the Lord. But the one who revealed it moved quickly, as that simple statement dictated.

The words of the Lord recorded in the red letter edition of the Bible will be fulfilled by you. Whether he quotes the Old Testament or relates to it, you are predestined to fulfill the red letters recorded there.

The entire drama has unfolded in me, so I know the perfect pattern that God sent into the world. We are told the first shall be last, and the last first. In the story the last act is recorded as the crucifixion yet it is the first. I have been crucified with Christ. It is not I who live, but Christ who lives in me. And the life I now live in the flesh I live by faith in the Son of God, who loves me and gave himself for me by actually becoming me. His name is I AM. That's the Lord God Jehovah, who is Christ. He is God the Father who became you. His death – in the sense of complete forgetfulness as to his true identity and belief that he is actually you – is your life. It is this being who tells you: "Unless I die thou canst not live, but if I die I shall rise again and thou with me." He rose in me. He proved that he could die and rise, for when he rose I rose knowing I AM He. He became me in the most intimate way by becoming my awareness. Then he talked to me and revealed himself to me from within my very self. In the beginning the words seemed to come from another, as though someone on the outside had spoken them; yet they were whispered from within as everything said of Jesus Christ unfolded in me.

Can you accept my words and keep the tense? It is so very important to do so, for if you turn to the second person, or the third, you have created a false God and a false Jesus Christ. Do you not realize that Jesus Christ is in you? For unless you believe that your I amness is He you will die in your sins. Put the little word 'is' in the sentence: "Unless you believe that I am is He, you die in your sins," to give it meaning, for without it you may think a being on the outside is speaking and keeping you from missing the mark. If you want to be rich and do not believe that you are the cause of wealth, then you will go on missing the mark by remaining poor. The true goal is to know God is your own wonderful human imagination. This God you will never lose, for when he reveals himself within you it is in a first person, present tense experience.

As God unfolds himself within you he doesn't call himself "God," but "I AM." It was "I" who awoke and rose in that tomb; no one else was there. I had no help getting out; "I" pushed the stone away myself. And when I looked back to see that out of which I came, I saw the three witnesses as recorded in Genesis. It is said that Abraham (the state of faith in which I started) was seated by the door of his tent in the heat of the day when the three men appeared. As one spoke concerning the child, Abraham knew he was the Lord. That child is Isaac, which means, "he laughs." I found that promised child. Like Simeon, I took that promised child in my arms and he laughed.

So who is Christ? And who is the Lord? Did scripture not fulfill itself in me? I have come only to fulfill scripture, and this I have done. I know I am the temple of the Living God, for my body was torn from top to bottom. I found my son, He who was set up in the beginning to reveal me as the Father. This is not what the priesthoods teach; but I am telling you what I have experienced, for I have found David. He cried unto me: "Thou art my Father."

I do not care what the priesthoods of the world may say; I am telling you what I know from experience. If they do not believe in me, they will continue to live in sin by worshipping a false God. All the priesthoods and rabbis worship an idol, for the true God cannot be worshipped in any tense other than the present. His name is I Am. No picture on a wall or statue in a garden is the Lord. "Make no graven image unto me." If you do not see him as yourself you will not find him, and when he comes he reveals himself through his son calling you Father. This you set up in the beginning and then you agreed to play all the parts. Not one part can you condemn, for all contribute to the end when you find God. The goal of life is to find him, not on the outside, but within yourself in the first person, present tense. The world thinks I am insane when I tell them who I am, for they see the garment of flesh I wear and know I am subject to all its weaknesses. But because the drama of the scripture has unfolded within me, I know how true scripture is.

I cannot describe the joy that is yours when you awaken. I can only say that the world into which I go night after night is entirely different, and earth does not contain anything which I can use as an image to describe that world. I return through darkness into this world every day to share my experiences with everyone who will listen, while some believe me and some do not. My most intimate friends may not believe me, for they know and judge me by my human weaknesses. My brothers, knowing we were sired by the same father and came out of the same mother's womb, cannot believe my experiences are related to scripture. But I am not asking you to believe in Neville, but to believe in God who is your own wonderful human awareness.

I have been sent to tell you who God is. He who sent me is one with me, for although he seemed to be another when I stood in his presence, when we embraced we fused and became one. The recording angel, the ledger, the being of love who embraced me, is within. In the beginning I foreknew myself. Through foreknowledge I was predestined to be called from the world of death, called from within myself by an infinite being of love, wearing the human form divine, to be embraced and sent. And the moment we embraced we fused, and I knew myself to be infinite love. There had been a seeming separation when I entered a world that was not mine, to experience all of its horrors until its end when I am called, acquitted, justified, and glorified. Now there is nothing left for me to do but tell it to everyone who will listen and urge them to set their entire hope upon this grace which is coming to all at the unveiling of Christ in each individual, in the first person, present tense.

While you are here you can become independently secure, certainly. All of these things are possible to you, but the real objective in your life is to find God, the cause of all life. To believe in God does not aid you. The question is: do you believe in yourself? Can you believe you are rich when you have no money? Can you continue to believe it throughout the day and fall asleep night after night as though you were? If you will, you will become rich. Then fulfill another desire and then another, and one day you will discover the one who made it possible. That one is God.

Millions of people claim to believe in God in the third person, but they do not know God. Only when God reveals himself in the first person, present tense can he be known. That God cannot be outgrown or lost, for you cannot outgrow I am. I am is the theme of the Book of John, which goes back to the 3rd chapter of the Book of Exodus, the 14th verse, as: "Go say, 'I am has sent me to you." As a man, I am revealing God's true name, but those who hear my words know the outer garment I wear and judge it. They know my weaknesses, but they do not know the Lord. I tell you: when you know the Lord (or rather are known by him) you will experience a thrill that is beyond description. Your shock will turn to joy, however, as the drama of one called Jesus Christ unfolds within you.

In the meantime you can test him in the world of Caesar. There is no limit to his power, so take that power which became you and attach it to your desire. Sleep every night so attached to your desire that you feel its reality, and in no time you will prove my words. Within a year the lady in New York City received her $50,000, pressed down and running over. She knew exactly what she did and would never have guessed that the little old lady she bought the paper for every Sunday morning would be used as the means to give her the wealth she claimed. This lady has found God, yet she is still inclined to speak of him in the third person.

Man is in the habit of thinking of God and not as God. It is so easy to forget to keep the tense. Every good, well-trained Jew is familiar with the first five books of the Old Testament. They have read the Book of Exodus many times and believe God is the great I AM; yet they still think of him in the third person. They would think that anyone who boldly stood up and proclaimed, "I Am He" was arrogant; yet I tell you that is the only way you will ever find God.

But when he comes, there is no need to brag about it. You know who you are, and when they call you by your earthly name you respond. Perhaps you will have dinner together, but they will continue to be totally unaware of the being within you, and you don't always throw pearls before swine, because they are not prepared to receive them. You will join their party and enjoy the evening as you let the outer man play his part, but you know the inner man, the one they know not of. That man is Jesus Christ.

There is only one Christ. Everyone has been crucified with that one Christ can make the statement: "It is not I who live, but Christ who lives in me. And the life I now live in this body of flesh and blood, I live by the faith of the Son of God, who loved me and gave himself for me." God actually became as you are, that you may rise to the one being called God the Father. As one power, we came down from God to become the gods. In order to descend in power and play these parts we had to enter complete forgetfulness. The actor cannot pretend. He must enter and become the part he has agreed to play. He cannot step upon the stage knowing he is a great actor who everyone recognizes. He must lose himself in the character by leaving his personality in the dressing room and entering the stage as the character he is to portray. So when God stepped upon the stage wearing this, he is Neville, one hundred per cent. He had to completely forget that he was God, yet knowing that he brought with him a pattern which would erupt and his memory would return. I agreed to play the part as Neville. He and I are one, but I am greater than he.

Look upon Jesus Christ as a pattern. I have told you how the pattern erupted in me in the hope that you will believe me. Although a few believe my words, the majority disbelieve fulfilling scripture. "He came unto his own and his own believed him not." What I tell you and what you are capable of conceiving may be entirely different. Can you receive what I tell you as my own personal experience? I can tell you that scripture is true from beginning to end, but can you believe me enough to set your hope fully upon the grace that is coming to you at the unveiling of God within you? I hope so, for God is in you as your I am. And when he awakes you go through a series of supernatural events called Jesus Christ. Then you will tell your experiences to those who will listen in the hope that they will accept them; but it does not matter if they do or do not, for in the end, you take off your garment of flesh and return to an intimacy that is indescribable.

Eyes have not seen or ears heard the things that are already prepared for you. In that world you are in control of everything and everything is alive. Every night I pass beyond the world of dream to enter the world of reality, and I return each morning through the world of dream to reenter this world of death. This I do night after night, and will continue to do until that moment in time when it pleases the depth of my own being (who is the Father) to take off this garment of flesh and call it a day.

Remember, you can only sin against that self of you who is God. And any time you think of God in any tense other than the first person, present, you are entertaining an idol, no matter what you call it. If you leave this auditorium tonight conscious of being God, you are walking in the knowledge of the true God and all things are possible to you. Walk in complete trust that things are as you want them to be. This is loyalty to unseen reality. This is faith. There are only two things that displease God: One is lack of faith in I AM He, and the other is eating of the tree of knowledge of good and evil.

Before descending into the land of forgetfulness you made yourself a promise that one day your memory would return and you would realize you were the creator of it all, for God gave you himself. He actually became you, as told in the story of Melchizedek. He had no father, no mother, no beginning, and no end. In the end you become a priest after the order of Melchizedek, knowing the whole vast infinite universe was created by and sustained by you. Now, this is really incredible. I recently read that the great Einstein said: "I rejoice in the discovery of the uniformity of the laws of nature and whoever is behind it that we call the Lord. But that man should survive the disintegration of the brain, to me is unthinkable." If a man as wonderful as Einstein feels that the story of the gospel is unthinkable, then condemn no one. You can't deny Einstein's greatness. He was tender, kind and sincere; but in spite of that gentility he was quite satisfied to dwell in the uniformity of the laws of nature and whoever is behind it.

I tell you there is one behind it all. He so loved you he became you and the day is coming when you will know that you are he. You will know you are not the creation of the city, but its creator. You are not the made, but the maker. Whether you are male or female, you are the emanation of the Lord yet his wife till the sleep of death is past. Then you will awake to know you never left your heavenly home, you were never born and never die, save in your dreams.

Now let us go into the silence.

Before Abraham, Was I Am

The drama tonight opens to the 8th chapter of the Book of John, where the evangelist writes of the state into which he has entered, saying: "Truly, truly I say to you, before Abraham, was I am."

The Bible is a recordation of the eternal spiritual states of the soul which everyone must pass through, beginning with the state of Abraham and culminating in the state called Jesus Christ. It is important, therefore, to distinguish between the man and the state he occupies at the present time.

Always remember that the Bible is address to the man of imagination and not to any mortal man. Blake said: "It must be understood that the persons Moses and Abraham are not here meant, but are states signified by those names. The individuals being representatives (or visions) of those states as they were seen by mortal man in a series of divine revelations and recorded in the Bible." I have seen these states in my imagination. At a distance they appeared as one man; however, as I drew near they became a multitude of nations. One man – represented by multitudes and multitudes of men in harmony – appears as a single being. The ancients saw Him and believing in what they saw they prophesied of the ultimate state, and personified him as Jesus Christ.

No one knows the true authors of Matthew, Mark, Luke and John, but I can tell you, they were relating their own experiences when they put words into the mouth of a personification of this ultimate truth called Jesus. Turning to those who were present he said: "Your father Abraham rejoiced that he was to see my day. He saw it and was glad." Those who heard him said: "Why, you are not yet fifty years of age, and Abraham saw you?" And he replied: "Before Abraham, was I am." With that remark they took up stones and stoned him.

Now this was not a drama that took place in the secular world. The evangelist is telling the truth, however, for being in the state of

Jesus Christ he knew he was the immortal being who was before Abraham. He knew he was God himself, the author of the play called life. This truth every child born of woman will know from experience.

Let us now turn to the Book of Galatians, which is the earliest book of the New Testament. The thirteen letters of Paul were written, distributed, practiced, and called the gospel at least twenty years before the gospels Matthew, Mark, Luke, and John were written. In it, Paul speaks of "my gospel," saying: "I did not receive it from a man, nor was I taught it, it came by revelation of Jesus Christ." Then he tells this story: "Abraham had two sons, one by a slave and one by a free woman. The son of the slave was born according to the flesh, the son of the free woman by the promise. This is an allegory: these two women are two covenants. The one who bears the child by promise is Jerusalem from above." This is the state called Sarah.

Paul states quite boldly here that the story of Abraham, Hagar, and Sarah is an allegory. And an allegory is a story told as if it were true, leaving the one who hears (or reads) it to discover its symbolic representation and learn its lesson. Hagar and Sarah symbolize two covenants, one bringing in slavery and one freedom.

My mother was not named Hagar and the chances are your mother was not either, but every woman who has a child – in the language of symbolism – is Hagar. The child may be born in a palace and his mother a queen. He may know enormous wealth and a life of ease, but he (or she) is still a slave. Whoever wears a garment of mortality must take care of it, for it assimilates and must expel, through some artifice, that which it cannot assimilate. Whether the garment be that of a queen or a scrubwoman, it enslaves its occupant. And no matter how strong the garment, it waxes and waxes until it reaches a peak and then it wanes and wanes and no one can stop its inevitable change and death. So every child born from the womb of woman is a slave.

But there is another birth – a birth into freedom – which is essential, for unless you are born from above you cannot enter the kingdom of God. And the womb from which that birth takes place is the human skull, called Jerusalem from above.

Blake identifies Jerusalem from above with liberty, for after this second birth one is liberated. Having been placed into a world of slavery and death, the second birth is our victory over death. Everyone will be victorious... but everyone! We came into this world of death, have fought the good fight, and will continue to fight it. We are running a race with our enemy, death, (in) which all will be victorious. Everyone will be resurrected. Everyone will be born from above and all will enter the kingdom of God.

Ask no man to describe the kingdom for you, as eyes have not seen, nor ears heard, nor has it entered into the hearts of men the things God has already prepared for those who enter that state. There are no images here on earth to aid you in trying to visualize that state, so let no man tell you he knows and can describe it to you, for it can't be done.

The New Testament begins: "The book of the genealogy of Jesus Christ, the son of David, the son of Abraham." If the story of Abraham is an allegory, then the end of the story – called Christ – must be an allegory, for it was established in the beginning that everything would bring forth after its own kind. A carrot seed contains within itself the capacity to become a carrot. An apple seed when planted will bring forth an apple tree, and so forth. So if the origin of any story is an allegory, the end is an allegory. Not knowing how to read scripture, man believes it is secular history and worships states, making mental pictures of them, painting and even sculpturing them; yet every character recorded there is only the personification of a state.

Let me share an experience of mine with you. In my vision I came upon a man in his fifties, about six feet tall, and looking as though he had an infinite capacity of faith. I didn't have to ask his name, for I recognized him instantly. (Wisdom from above is without uncertainty. When you come upon these states in vision, you know who they are). The moment I saw him, I knew I was looking at the state called Abraham. He was standing erect, yet leaning somewhat against the trunk of what looked like an oak tree totally devoid of leaves. Its branches were curled and knotted, resembling the human brain. Twisted around the trunk of the tree was a serpent with a human face, bathed in wisdom and the symbol of the final state called Christ. Abraham was looking – not into space, but time, and I wondered what this wisest of all of God's creatures had whispered into his ear.

Paul personifies scripture by saying: "The scriptures foreseeing that God would justify the Gentiles, preached the gospel beforehand to Abraham." The scriptures must be personified in order to preach. So three thousand years before the coming of Christ, Abraham was given a preview of God's plan of salvation in the form of the gospel. Therefore, Abraham rejoiced that he was to see my day; he saw it and was glad.

When I say "I" (or "my") I mean "we," for we are the gods who collectively form God. In the great play, God is fragmented and the one becomes the many. But before the state of Abraham we – in perfect unity – wrote the play for a divine purpose. We agreed to enter the world of death and completely forget who we are in order to make the play real. This we have done and we will return enhanced by the play, but we cannot stop half way or turn back, we must finish the race. Everyone will fight the good fight. Everyone will go to the end and keep the faith we began in the state called Abraham.

The tree I saw was a perfect symbol of the tree of life. In Blake's "Songs of Experience," he said: "The gods of the earth and sea sought through nature to find that tree. But their search was all in vain, there grows one in the human brain." That's where the tree of life is. Having been felled, its roots are inverted in the brain with its branches as man's nervous and circulatory systems. Man is the inverted tree, like the one you would see reflected in the still waters of a lake. Turned down into generation, that tree symbolized as man, will be turned up from generation to regeneration. On that day man is resurrected and returns, bringing back the fruit (the experiences) of this great play of decay and death.

So Abraham is not a person as you are, as I am, any more than Isaac, Jacob, David, and all the others are persons. They are personifications of the eternal states of the soul. So if the origin called Abraham and the fulfillment called Jesus Christ are an allegory, then the fruit (glorious as it is) is also an allegory. And you will reap it to return greater than the being you were when you came out from the Father and came into the world, and no one will be lost... not one.

In the kingdom, however, we will play different parts, just as we play them here. Although sharing one body, one Spirit, one Lord, one God and Father of all, there are ranks in the kingdom just as there are ranks in the army. Those who fill the stars of the crown do so not by merit, but by election – which remains a secret of the Most High. But remember: the least in the kingdom is greater than the greatest on earth. "I would rather be a doorkeeper in the house of the Lord than live in the house of the wicked." Well, a doorkeeper may be on the threshold, but he is in the kingdom. We are told that no one born of woman is greater than John the Baptist, yet the least in the kingdom is greater than he.

No matter how great, wise, strong, or handsome one is here on earth, he is less than the least in the kingdom of God. So do not be concerned as to what part you play in the body of God, for the least part is greater than anything on earth. In the third great act of God's awakening, you reenter the kingdom violently to discover your position. Entering the body of the Risen Lord like a bolt of lightening, you are the cause of its reverberation, and your entrance denotes your position. There will be no menial parts there, for all will be a necessary part of the body of the Risen Lord.

So, before Abraham, was I am. That is God's name forever and by this name he shall be known by all generations. God preceded his play, so the evangelist is telling the truth when he says, before Abraham, was I am.

Dwell on the words I have given you tonight. Know how truly great you are, then allow everyone to play their parts perfectly. If someone tells you he wants to feel important, let him feel it. If he wants to make an impression, let him make it. He is playing a part in the world of Caesar and maybe he has to make that impression for a certain self-satisfaction as he passes through the state. If you look at a person spiritually you can see the spiritual state he is in and realize that while he is in the state, he is playing his part perfectly.

We are all immortal beings who pass through states until we reach the state of Jesus Christ, the state designating the end of the journey. And when you enter that state scripture unfolds in you, casting you in the role of the central character and you are awed and thrilled. Prior to that moment in time you would have thought it blasphemy to claim such divinity, but when it happens you can no more deny it than you can the simplest evidence of your senses. And having experienced scripture, you have fulfilled the only purpose of life and you know it.

All of the stories of the Bible are supernatural truths which take place in a remote region of the soul. A lady here tonight said: "As I examined a translucent box covered with skin, you appeared and began to peel transparent skin from your cheeks." She saw correctly. At the end of the journey the skin you wear – which was so responsive to the inner you, that you thought you were it – will be taken off, and your true identity revealed.

I have a little namesake in New Your City. His name is Neville Mark. I saw him a month before he was born and when I asked when he was coming on earth he answered quite innocently: "The tenth of November." A very dear friend of ours was pregnant at the time and expecting her child in December. I shared my experience with her and told her that should her baby be born on the tenth of November and he was a boy, his name was Neville Mark. Well, even though she did not believe me, her baby arrived on the tenth of November and she named him Neville Mark. About three or four years ago I visited the family, and Neville Mark – twelve or thirteen at the time – said to me: "Neville, I know that I am not what I appear to be. If I could only get my body to stand perfectly still while I turn around in it, I would know who I am. I also know I cannot do it until I die, and I can hardly wait to learn my true identity."

This little lad knew what my friend saw, for he knew that the skin which was tightly woven over him hid his true identity. This is true, for everyone here is wearing a mask. One day the mask will be taken off and we will all meet unmasked, yet we will know each other as we did before Abraham. There will be one grand, wonderful, joyous moment when– having returned – we recognize the being we were prior to putting on our masks to play the play of life.

The evangelist knew from his own experience that before the state called Abraham was I am, yet those who heard his story took up stones to throw at him. Now, a stone symbolizes a literal fact. The stones they threw were the facts of his life here on earth. They knew his parents, his brothers and sisters, as well as his educational and social background. They knew he was not yet fifty, yet he was speaking of one who was recorded to have lived two thousand years ago.

Friends here have thrown the same facts at me. I recall one night at a dinner party I told the late Aldous Huxley that these characters were not persons, and he said: "Neville, Caesar and Herod lived and they are mentioned in scripture." And I replied: "I speak of the scripture which is the Old Testament, and they are not there. If you want to accept Jesus as a man, the only book he could have read was the Old Testament. In the temple he was given the book and read the words of the prophet Isaiah. Everything he quoted was from the Old Testament, as the New hadn't been written."

I am not denying that Paul and the evangelists lived, but they are anonymous. The Old Testament is a recordation of eternal states, and the prophets who recorded them were doing a work the full import of which they did not understand. They inquired as to what time or person was meant, and it was revealed to them that they were serving not themselves, but us.

When the time fully comes, the secret will be uncovered and we will see the end, as we fulfill the state called Jesus Christ. Each will enter it, one after the other, and all will experience everything that is recorded in the scripture concerning Jesus Christ. And when each one of us has had the identical experience, who are we? Are we not Jesus Christ, the perfect man who reflects the glory of God and bears the very stamp of his person!

When you reach that state the work is done and you return to where you were before your deliberate fall. You did nothing wrong, but took the challenge, for only God could die in confidence that he would rise. We are the gods who took the challenge, who came down and entered these masks that decay and die, to find ourselves restored, waxing once more, waning, and dying. Restored, waxing, waning, and dying, over and over and over until the end is reached. Then there is no more restoration – only resurrection – as we are lifted out of the world of death to enter the kingdom of heaven, the world of life.

Everyone is destined to be in that kingdom, to play his predetermined part, for "Those whom he foreknew he predestined to be conformed to the image of his son, and those whom he predestined he called, and those whom he called he justified, and those whom he justified he glorifies." Everyone, even the least in the kingdom, will be glorified in the body of the Risen Lord and remember: before Abraham, was I am.

Now let us go into the silence.

I Am In You

As Paul said to Timothy: "Great indeed, we confess, is the mystery of our religion." Scripture is not secular history, but a mystery which is most important that we understand!

Speaking to his disciples, Jesus said: "In that day you will know that I am in the Father, and you in me and I in you."[1] The phrase "in that day" is an eschatological term meaning, "at the end of the journey." In other words, when this age of Caesar comes to its end, you will experience the truth of scripture, and – understanding – you will say: "I am in the Father and you are in me and I am in you."

It is in you, as a person, that the nature of God reveals himself in a series of supernatural experiences. When these take place in a first person, singular, present tense experience, all arguments, doubts, and questions regarding your true identity are hushed. From that moment on, like Paul, you will say: "When it pleased God to reveal his son in me, I conferred not with flesh and blood. I did not receive my gospel from a man. I was not taught it. It came through a revelation of Jesus Christ.

While in Barbados this summer, my sister asked if my Christ was once a man. My answer to her undoubtedly was the same Paul gave when asked a similar question. I said: "Was? He is the heavenly man!" Then quoting Paul I said: "Just as we have borne the image of the man of dust, we shall also bear the image of the man of heaven."

Do not think of Christ as some little boy who was born in some strange manner two thousand years ago. We are dealing with a cosmic principle, where God actually became man that man may become God.

---

[1] John 14

21

The process has started. Resurrection has begun, but it is not over. Those who teach that the resurrection is over are misleading the faithful, for – like Paul – everyone can say: "I have been crucified with Christ. It is not I who live, but Christ who lives in me. The life I now live in the flesh, I live by the faith of the son of God who loved me and gave himself for me. Henceforth I regard no one from a human point of view. Even though I once regarded Christ from a human point of view, I regard him thus no longer."

I have stood in the presence of the Risen Lord. I leave seen the Ancient of Days, who is gathering us one by one into his body to become one body, one Spirit, one Lord, one God and Father of all.

You, as a person, will not be less than the Risen Lord, for there is only one Spirit. There is only one Lord and you will know yourself to be He! No one will be above you. I AM the same body, the same Lord, the same Spirit, the same God and Father of all. Without loss of identity, we will all know ourselves to be this one unity of being. We will know from experience that I AM in you and you are in me!

When I had finished explaining this to Daphne, I don't think she was any more impressed than that chair over there. It takes time, but it is so important for you to let go of all intermediaries between yourself and God!

Paul's Letter to the Galatians is the first book in the New Testament. In this letter, Paul declares his independence from men and his dependence upon God. He repudiates all authorities, all institutions, all customs, all laws that interfere with the individual's direct access to his God. Paul had no intermediary. He never knew a human Christ, only the Risen Lord, who appeared to him as he appeared to me.

In my own case, I was taken in Spirit into the presence of the Risen Lord, and – strangely enough – when he asked me what was the greatest thing in the world, I answered in the words of Paul. So I ask you: who is Paul? Is he not the first of the chosen who broke the seal and discovered the mystery which was shown to Abraham?

Paul persecuted everyone who claimed to be a member of the way, when suddenly the revelation broke, causing him to proclaim the truth. It was Paul who said: "If I have been united with Christ in a death like his, I shall certainly be united with him in a resurrection like his."

Paul did not claim that the resurrection was over. He states that the crucifixion is over, because the garment of flesh is worn by one who is crucified. God chose you in him before the foundation of the world. We will be united with him in a resurrection like his – not because of any acquired merit on our part, but because he chose to be united to us in a death like his.

You were chosen in him before the drama we call the world began. And any suffering you may go through here means nothing. Paul knew this, and said: "I consider the sufferings of the present time not worth comparing to the glory which is to be revealed in us."

Now, the Old Testament tells us: "In the beginning was the Word, and the Word was with God and the Word was God. The Word became flesh and dwells in us." The Greek word logos (translated as "Word") means "meaning; a plan; a plot; a purpose." Here we see that God had a plan, a purpose – which was to give himself to you one hundred per cent. This he has done; so whatever he was before he became you, you will know yourself to be.

It is in you, as a person, that the nature of God reveals himself. This you will know when you experience the entire story of the Lord Jesus Christ in the first person, present tense. Then when you tell those who love you, they will not believe you, because they know your weaknesses and limitations.

Knowing you are not schooled in theology, they cannot see the relationship between you and the one spoken of in the seventh chapter of John: "How does this man have such learning seeing as how he has never studied?" Like the Sanhedrin, they will not understand how a man with no learning could claim that the Old Testament had been fulfilled in him.

The prophets foretold of the coming of God, but they did not say how. Having taken upon himself man's nature, God unfolds his nature in man, and man becomes God. If God was a father prior to choosing you, and he becomes you – are you not a father? Yes, but there is no way to prove this, unless God's son appears to identify you. Only when God's son unfolds within you, will you know that you are God.

Only the Risen Christ is aware of his true identity. It is he who says: "I am in you and you are in me, Lo we are one." The Risen Christ is the eternal heavenly man, who is God. You are a man. Learn to adore your own humanity, who is God. Man is looking for some impersonal force to worship, but God is man!

When I stood in his presence, I answered his question in the words of Paul. Since then I have asked myself: who is Paul? Was he not the beginner of the Christian faith? Our New Testament records thirteen of his letters, all written twenty years prior to the gospels.

In his first letter to the Galatians, Paul went out on a limb by declaring his independence from all organizations. That was in the day when you could not get a job unless you were a member of the synagogue; yet Paul refused to accept any intermediary between himself and the Risen Lord, whom he had persecuted in his blindness.

One day the Risen Christ will bring you into his presence. He will incorporate you into his body by an embrace from which you will be one forever and ever. This I know from experience.

So when I tell you I am in you, I mean it literally, for I am one with the Risen Christ. I am speaking the words of the Risen Christ, not Neville. After we embraced, he sent me, yet he has never separated himself from me. How can I be one with the body who sent me? Because "He who sees me, sees him who sent me."

Limited to the concept of three-dimensional space, we think of being sent out of the room while the sender remains; but in the Spirit world of which I speak, when one is united with the Lord he becomes one with him in spirit.

Dwell upon this being who became you. Return to the point of being chosen before that the world was. Try to remember when he made known unto you the mystery of his plan which gives meaning to your life — this mystery which was set forth in Christ for the fullness of time.

The Word, giving meaning to the world, was with God and was God. That meaning is Christ, a plan which cannot fail to fulfill its purpose, which is to unfold and reveal you as God. Walking this earth right now, you are God's Word, moving towards fulfillment.

Now, while we are here waiting for God's plan to unfold, we should continue to apply God's law. Here is a simple story. My friend wrote, saying: "When my little boy was quite young, as a family we called the Sears' Christmas catalog, the "Wish Book". Our son would spend hours looking through the pages of toys, deciding what he wanted for Christmas. This we have done for the past eight years. I am enclosing a card advertising the current issue of that catalog. As you will see, it is now called "The Sears Wish Book!"

Whoever has that account thinks this is an original idea, yet my friend knows she is its creator. You see, there is no fiction. How can there be fiction in a world where imagining creates reality? For eight years her son has known the catalog to be a wish book, and now that has become its official name. If something you have imagined is delayed producing its reality for you, keep this story in mind.

I know we are all children and want our desires instantly fulfilled, but countries plan for unborn generations. Parents with large estates plan, not only for the present little ones, but for the offsprings of their offsprings.

You and I, however, are anxious and find it difficult to wait. Time and time again, ladies have told me they wanted to be married now, only to confess they are not yet divorced. I have heard them say there was only one man.

Either that man or no man, yet they have married another. What they really wanted was to be happily married. Claiming it had to be that man, I have asked: "If he dropped dead right now would you still have the urge for companionship? If you would, then he is not the only man."

Know what you want in life and do not condition it. If your desire is to be happily married, claim you are. Wanting a certain home, claim you have it. Don't think you cannot afford it, simply play the wishing game.

Find your desire in God's wish book. Speaking to you through the medium of desire, make your desire real by feeling its truth. View the world from its fulfillment. Lose yourself in the feeling of possession and give it all the tones of reality. Fulfill every desire as you walk towards the fulfillment of your real purpose in life, which is to awaken God in you.

You are not going to become a little god to run around with other little gods, for there is only one God. Don't forget the great Sh'ma: "Hear O Israel, the Lord our God, the Lord is one." You are destined to awaken as that one God and Father of all.

When I awoke in this simple little thing called man, I wondered how this mortal being could bear such responsibility. Housed in this garment of flesh called Neville, aware of all of its weaknesses, God's purpose has unfolded; yet I have no way to prove it to anyone.

I cannot convince you unless you have faith. I have shared my experiences in the written form, giving passages of scripture to support them. Having reached the end of the journey, I now know from experience that we enter human history to fulfill scripture.

I tell you: the story of Christ is an acted parable, a story told as if it were true, leaving the one who hears (or reads) it to discover the fictitious character and learn its meaning.

In the parable the actor takes a little child in his arms and says: "This is the kingdom of heaven. Unless you accept the kingdom as a little child, you cannot enter it." One day you will be that actor, and the little child in your arms will symbolize your entrance into heaven. It is a signal of God's birth – not from the womb of a woman, but from the skull of man, where God is crucified. His name is I AM. And when you awaken you will say, I AM awake. You will not look around for any other, for you will be alone; and from then on scripture will fulfill itself within you.

In the not distant future you will depart this world to discover that death will force you to modify, or radically change, any ideas which you have championed here. I received a notice today that my good friend, Randy, died. In 1952, while recuperating from a serious operation, Randy came to the hospital to visit me. He was my physician as well as my friend, but was not aware of what I teach. Seeing the Bible I had brought with me, Randy questioned my interest in it.

Taking the story of Esau and Jacob, I told him how Esau represented my outer world. That I could close my eyes to it and clothe Jacob (who represented what I wanted clothed in outer reality) with the skins of Esau. Believing in the reality of what I am doing, I deceive myself into believing that my subjective state is now an objective reality.

Well, to Randy that was not religion. To him religion meant going to church every Sunday morning and spending an hour there. That was something to be done, like walking with a cane because you had one and felt undressed without it. His week was not complete unless he went to church on Sunday. Randy has been gone now a few weeks and, undoubtedly is now modifying his beliefs – but it will take time.

You do not awaken there as some wise person. If you are foolish here, you are foolish there. If you are a thief here, you are a thief there. If a man is not a thief, no matter what is put before him he would not take it; therefore there is no temptation, no desire to change. Place all the liquor in the world before a man who does not drink and he will not be tempted. All of the world's tobacco will not interest a man who does not smoke, therefore there is no temptation.

When a man is regenerated, he is no longer in the world of generation. Everyone could undress before him, yet he would not be tempted, because his energies have been turned up into regeneration.

Everyone will be regenerated and overcome without effort, for when the visions happen, you change. Change does not occur prior to the visions, because fitness is the consequence – not the condition – of the kingdom of heaven. You are not chosen because of your acquired merit. The minute the vision takes place, the consequence has occurred.

When you read the words of Christ in the New Testament, think of the Risen Christ, for the heavenly man is speaking. We are all rising into the one body of Christ without loss of identity. I will know you better and more intimately there than I could ever know you here, for the mask we wear here causes a barrier between us. But in the New Age we will be intimate eternal brothers, all sharing the one body as the one Spirit, the one Lord, the one God and Father of all.

Now let us go into the silence.

I Am *the* Cause

According to a rabbical principle, that which is not written in scripture is non-existent. The story of Jesus Christ follows this principle.

The unknown author of the Book of Luke (like all the others) wrote only of his own experiences. Turning to his disciplined mind in self contemplation, he is Jesus turning to his disciples and saying: "'Scripture must be fulfilled in me. All that is written about me must be fulfilled.' Beginning with Moses and the prophets, and the psalms he interpreted to them in all the scriptures the things concerning himself. And they said to one another, 'Did not our hearts burn while he opened to us the scriptures?' Then he said to them, 'Everything written about me in the law of Moses and the prophets and the psalms must be fulfilled.' Then he opened their minds to understand the scriptures." Luke is speaking of the Christ in you, for any Christ coming from without is a false Christ, taught by false teachers.

Peter tells us: "Scoffers will come in the last days scoffing and saying, 'Where is the promise of his coming? Forever since the fathers fell asleep, all things have continued as they were from the beginning of creation.'" Certainly they do. Graft, war, dirty politics, poverty – you name it, everything will continue forever in this age; so do not look for signs of his coming in the outer world, as this age will continue producing poverty, graft, war, and unlovely things. But when Christ comes it is like a thief in the night. When you least expect it, Christ awakens within you to reveal yourself to yourself.

"In many and various ways God spoke of old to our fathers by the prophets, but in these last days he has spoken to us by his Son," for when the Son appears he reveals God as his Father. Until God's son reveals himself in Man, Man searches on the outside to discover how things are made, but he cannot find the Maker. Our world is God's handiwork, as told us in the 19th Psalm: "The heavens declare the glory of God and the firmament shows forth his handiwork." Our scientists have discovered how to go to the moon, from which they returned with earth. Then they analyzed it and discovered it to be dead. No matter where man goes, he will discover that everything is dead, for God's handiwork is here and here alone. But, no matter how much his handiwork is analyzed, it will not reveal its maker.

Today three of our citizens received the Nobel Prize for their great work in trying to analyze this wonderful land of ours. They will find many wonderful things about it, but they will never find its maker. He comes only when the individual finds the Son, for it is God's Son who reveals his maker. I tell you: the Bible is all about you. It is your own personal, spiritual biography. Every child born of woman is recorded in the Bible – not as John Brown or Mary Smith – but as Jesus Christ; for he is the child's true being, and the Old Testament is a prophetic blueprint of his life.

When you read the 9th chapter of Isaiah, you may wonder what it is all about, but may I tell you nothing could be truer. Listen carefully: "To us a child is born, to us a son is given; and the government shall be upon his shoulder, and his name shall be called `Wonderful Counselor, Mighty God, Everlasting Father, Prince of Peace." These revelations do not come in the order the prophets recorded them (or some scribe changed); but the names are true and are revealed in perfect order.

The first name given to you when you fell asleep was "El Shaddai" which means "God Almighty, or Mighty God". But one day you will awaken! Now completely individualized, you will feel a vibration so great you will think you are going to die; but far from dying, the vibration will awaken you from your long, long sleep. You will awaken within yourself to discover that you have been entombed there for unnumbered centuries. You may not know how you got there and why, but I'll tell you: you went voluntarily. No one took your life, you laid it down yourself.

You have the power to lay it down and the power to lift it up again. You deliberately entered the human skull and laid yourself down to dream the dream of life. Mystics claim you have been dreaming there for 6000 years. I have had no vision to support such a time interval, but I can say that when it happened to me I felt as though I had been entombed for unnumbered ages. For a moment I wondered how I got there, and then I remembered scripture: "He is not dead, but sleepeth, I go to awaken him." One day you, too, will hear the voice of the Son of God and awaken from your sleep of death, for when God sends his Son into your heart crying, "Father," you will hear it and awaken from your long, self-imposed sleep.

It takes an enormous power for Mighty God to stir himself and awaken to find the symbol of his birth as that of a child. You may think the child that is born and the son which is given are one and the same, but they are not. The son appears 139 days later. It is he who reveals you as God, the Maker and creator of it all. Prior to that moment in time you – like a scientist – look outside of yourself for the cause of all life; but when David – God's only begotten son – comes from within and calls you Father, you have found the cause. And when your son reveals you as the Father, the cause of all life, you will bear the name Everlasting Father.

Now, the third great revelation is that of Wonderful Counselor. And in scripture the Wonderful Counselor is associated with a serpent. Referred to as the wisest of all of God's creations, it was the serpent who suggested eating of the tree of knowledge. And when told he would die, the serpent said; "No, you will not truly die. For God knows that when you eat of it your eyes will be opened and you will be like God, knowing good and evil." The Wonderful Counselor did not lie, for believing himself to be you, he experienced death but did not really die.

Even though we depart this world and seem to die, we don't. Instead we are restored to life in a world just like this, to continue our journey for unnumbered centuries.

Now, in the same 3rd chapter of Genesis, the Lord said to the gods: "Behold the man has become like one of us, knowing good and evil," just as the serpent said he would. Only by coming down into this world of experience can you eat of the tree of knowledge of good and evil and become as the gods. So we see the 3rd title, Wonderful Counselor, has much to do with the serpent. We are told that: "No one ascends into heaven but he who descended from heaven, the son of man; and as Moses lifted up the serpent in the wilderness, so must the son of man be lifted up." When you read these words they do not make sense, but when you experience them – and you will – the third title of Wonderful Counselor is conferred upon you.

Your eyes will be opened then, and you will know good and evil from experience. You will know that you will not die, but will return to the heavenly state from which you – the son of man – descended. And you will ascend like a fiery serpent.

Now, the serpent of scripture is described in the 6th chapter of the Book of Isaiah as the seraphim which surround the throne of God. The seraphim is, by definition, a fiery being with human face, human voice, and human hands. Isaiah gives him six wings: two to cover his face, to cover his feet (which is a euphemism for his creative organs) and he flies with two; but beyond that, this heavenly being, the wisest of all God's creations, is not described. This is your true identity, for you are the gods who came down.

You are not some little amoeba which came out of the mud; you came down from heaven and emptied yourself of all that you were in order to assume the limitations and weaknesses of the human flesh. You are not pretending that you are man; you became man by assuming poverty, though you were rich. You assumed weakness, though you were strong. You – an infinite being – assumed all these things for their experience. The whole vast world declares your glory, but only here on this little earth is this wonderful work revealed.

Before we came here we were brothers, and one day we will awaken and return to our brotherhood as God the Father, of which it takes all of the brothers to form.

Now the 4th title, Prince of Peace, is sent in the form of a dove. This does not physically happen to you, and when it happens you are the only one who knows it. Read the first chapter, the 10th verse of the Gospel of Mark carefully, and you will see that only the one upon whom the dove descended was aware of it: "When he came up out of the water, immediately he saw the heavens open and the Spirit descended upon him like a dove." You are destined to have this experience as the fourth title, the Prince of Peace, is conferred upon you. You will bear the four titles, and in so doing you will fulfill scripture. Having foretold it you came down to fulfill it within yourself.

The testimony of Jesus is the Spirit of prophecy, and the name by which he is called is the Word of God. He is God's word which cannot return to God empty, but must accomplish that which he purposed and prosper in the thing for which it was sent. You are God's word which was in the beginning. You were not only with God, you were God. Then you fragmented into many sons, and it takes all of the sons to form the Father.

You came into this world to experience its horrors, not to change them. Our politicians promise to eliminate war and poverty, yet admit that they have sold over 13 billion dollars in conventional arms to poverty-ridden nations, as have the communist world. Our politicians have forced nations who can't afford to feed themselves, to buy what we are manufacturing.

Then, with a pious look, ask people to sign papers to stop war. But you can't stop it. This world was never intended to be other than what it is: a world of poverty, a world of war, a world of dirty politics, a world of graft. Just read the papers and you will see what is taking place in high places. You aren't going to change it; it will go on and on because the story of Christ is one of redemption. He redeems himself by lifting himself out of this world in a spiral motion.

This world is based upon a circular principle which repeats itself over and over again, whereas redemption is based upon a spiral principle. Breaking away from the wheel of recurrence, one moves up in a spiral motion – like the seraphim – and is redeemed. We are told that: "As the lightening shines from the east to the west so will the coming of the son of man."

People are looking for lightening to strike on the outside, but it strikes within. Your head is the Mount of Olives, and your body is that which is split from east to west. One half moves north as one half moves south, leaving a great valley. At the base of your spine you will see a pool of golden, liquid, pulsing light which is the blood of God. Fusing with it, you ascend into your skull like a fiery serpent and your skull reverberates like thunder.

I am telling you what you are going to experience, whether you can accept it or not and I know that you will never disprove it. I have awakened you, momentarily, but you may fall back to sleep again and continue your dream, of which you are its sole author.

It's very easy to be caught up in the reality that you, yourself, are making, even though what you see may frighten you.

You may have many horrors in your dream and believe what you are seeing is a reality outside of yourself and beyond your control, but you alone are writing the script. Haven't you had a dream where you were scared to death, not knowing you were its cause? The same thing is happening in the waking dream, but man does not know that this, too, is a dream, until he awakes from it in the manner of which I have told you.

One night as you sleep, something will arouse you and you will awaken to find yourself in your skull. You know it is your grave, where only the dead are placed; but you know yourself to be very much alive. Someone must have thought you dead to have placed you there, or you may have entered the place voluntarily and fell asleep to such depth that others thought you were dead. But when the time was fulfilled you heard the cry of the son of God which awakened you, and as you come out of that tomb you are born from above. This is essential, for unless you are born from above you cannot enter the kingdom of God.

Everyone is in this world because he is born from below (from the womb of woman), but while here he must be born from above (from the skull). That which comes out has no mother, no father, no beginning of days, or ending of days; for that which is born from the skull is aware of being the Maker of all. You will discover this great truth only when God's son stands before you and reveals you to yourself.

This tiny planet appears as only a speck when viewed from outer space, yet it is so important; for only here can this biological experiment which expands the power of God and the wisdom of God be cradled. Without this world, God could not grow in wisdom. He would be stagnant if he could not expand beyond what he is. God is an ever increasing illumination, an ever increasing creative power, an ever increasing wisdom and – by reason of this one little speck called earth, where he wears these little garments of mortality – God is holding to the promise he made himself: to awaken within himself and fulfill the play recorded in scripture.

The story of Christ is not what the world is talking about. He isn't going to change the world. Tomorrow's generation may think it will be different, but poverty will exist then as it does now. There will be changes in passion and eventually they will return to what they were. It's like a wheel. It's a circular principle where nothing changes. The individual changes only when he leaves the wheel in a spiral motion, and that is when he is redeemed. He returns to the world from which he came, enhanced by reason of his experience of death in this world called earth.

The principle of the rabbis is true, so let me repeat it: What is not written in scripture is non-existent. The presidents, kings, and dictators of the world are not recorded in scripture; therefore they are nonexistent. They are merely parts God is playing as he passes through states. The part of a president, a king, or a dictator is a state, and when entered it is animated. It seems so real to its occupant and to those who observe it, but it is only a state.

You can play any part – be it a rich man or a poor man, a beggar or a thief, the known or unknown – once you know they are only parts, only states of consciousness. But if you don't know this, and are not willing to give up your present state, you will remain there, looking at your desire and not from it. You can become what you would like to be in the twinkle of an eye by the simple act of assumption.

And the day you dare to remain faithful to your assumption, it will begin to externalize itself. And when it does you may return to sleep, just as you do in your night dreams. Becoming possessed by the dream you created in your sleep, you observe your own creation; and if it is a noble dream, you can become so puffed up in your own concept that you forget its creator. Or you can create something ignoble and become so immersed in it you believe in its reality. Anything can be created by a mere assumption. When I dared to assume I was the man I wanted to be, I did not discuss it with others; I simply persisted in my assumption and watched it harden into fact. That persistent act taught me that this world was a dream.

My oldest brother at the age of 18 had no money and no prospects of getting any. But he had a dream. He dreamed of owning a building which housed the family business. Twice a day, on his way to work and return, he would stop opposite a building which occupied an entire block at the widest area of the main street, and there he would imagine seeing the words: Goddard and Sons" on its marquee.

He persisted in this act for two years, when one day a total stranger bought the building for the family, trusting them to pay him back over a period of ten years. That building, which became the foundation of our family's growth, started in my brother's imagination. Having nothing on the outside to turn to, my brother had the guts to imagine and believe that his imagination would create his reality. Today I don't think you could buy the family out for multiple millions, because their gross business last year exceeded $30 million.

Do as my brother did and discover the depth of God in you. Test your imagination, for there is no other God. If you test him and discover that it is he who creates all things by producing tangible proof of his reality in what you did, then no one will be able to persuade you that what happened was a coincidence.

My brother lived by and built his fortune on imagination's foundation. Of course, having created such a vast enterprise he may go to sleep and believe his one thousand employees are the cause of his incredible wealth. We are all inclined to forget that we are the makers of all that is happening, and – forgetting – we blame our dream. The world is yourself pushed out; but it is so easy to place the blame on an aspect of self rather than on you, the dream's maker.

Learn to use your imagination consciously, for it will not fail you on this level or on the higher level. But you cannot depart this world by changing your thoughts. It will happen in the fullness of time, when the Father in you who fell asleep begins to stir. Then he awakens you, and when he does, you – Mighty God – will receive the name and carry the special powers of Everlasting Father, Wonderful Counselor, and Prince of Peace. And of your reign there shall be no end, for you will know yourself to be the Jesus Christ men worship outwardly.

The ministers of this world are talking about His coming, trying to interpret signs on the outside. But I tell you, Jesus does not come at the end of human history, for he comes individually. Tonight one of you could experience his coming. No one knows but the Father in you. Ever since that Father fell asleep all things have continued as they were from the beginning of creation. So don't look for any change on the outside.

When the politicians promise change, don't argue; smile as you have through the centuries, knowing they aren't going to change anything. The world is made up of infinite states which man falls into unwittingly – or deliberately, as my brother did. He was a poor boy who deliberately moved into the state of wealth. Not knowing how it was going to come about, he simply persisted in his assumption and it hardened into fact.

Do you like what the mirror reflects back to you and your background tells you? If it is not what you would like to live with, don't accept it. Rather, look into the mirror of your mind and assume that you are what you would like to be. Declaring that you are now it, don't look away and forget the image reflected there, but persist in your assumption. Live in that awareness morning, noon and night as though it were true, and no power can stop you from experiencing its truth.

This is a world of effects, as told us in the Book of James. If you look into the mirror and, seeing yourself, you turn away and forget what manner of man you look like, you will continue to perpetuate your unlovely state. But if you look into the mirror of your mind and – seeing what you desire to see, continue thinking from that state, you will see it reflect itself in your world. Then one day you will depart the world and return to the world from which you descended, for you are the Elohim, the God spoken of in the scriptures.

Do not be afraid to claim your birthright. An outside God never existed; therefore, don't make little images of him and stick them on your wall to worship. Is there any cross or image of Jesus Christ in the world that wasn't made by a man?

There is no description of a person called Jesus Christ, yet there are unnumbered pictures of him throughout the Christian world and people bow before that which is made by human hands. Read the 115th Psalm and see what the psalmist said about any image bowed to as some power that can help or hinder: "They have mouths, but do not speak; eyes, but do not see. They have ears, but do not hear; noses, but do not smell. They have hands, but do not feel; feet, but do not walk; and they do not make a sound out of their throat. Those who make them are like them; so are all who trust in them." If anyone should say: "Look, there he is, or here he is," believe him not; for when the Father of all life appears, you shall know him because you will be one with him!

The Bible is all about you, and you are here in the final picture to fulfill that which you dictated before you came down. The prophets you inspired were only organs of revelation. And God's son, by his very nature reveals God as his father. So when God's only begotten son stands before you and reveals you as his father, are you not God the Father? This I know from personal experience. I am not speculating. I am not theorizing. I did not hear it from a man, nor was I taught it.

Like Paul, it came through a revelation of the true meaning of Jesus Christ. It's all in scripture and everyone will experience it. And when we take off these garments and rise, you and I – as the brothers who have returned – will be in a state of ecstasy, for we will all have the same son. If your son is my son, and our son is his son, are we not one father? There aren't multiple sons – only one. We are all individualized. We will never lose our individuality, yet we are one in spirit because we have the one son; therefore we are brothers who collectively form God the Father.

Scripture is based upon the principle that the True Man comes here to fulfill. All that is said about the True you in the law of Moses and the prophets and the psalms, must and will be fulfilled. It is my pleasure and my privilege to open your mind that you may understand scripture. That is all I am here to tell you. But you will never really understand my words until you experience them, and you will.

There is no aristocracy of privilege in this story. We are all one! One is no better than the other. I have awakened from the dream of life. Now I only wait for others to awaken. There is nothing I want more than the awakening of all, because without all, the Father is not complete. So I tell my story over and over until everyone hears it and sets their hope fully upon this wonderful story that one day must erupt within them.

Now let us go into the silence.

I Am *the* Lord

"**I** am the LORD and there is no other. I form light and create darkness. I make weal and create woe. I, the LORD, do all these things."[2] Then John tells us, "As He is, so are we in this world." Although man is taught the God who creates the weal and the woe is someone other than himself, scripture tells us that as God is, so are we!

The story of Jesus Christ, as well as all of the miracles recorded in the New Testament, are acted parables. In the Book of Luke we find Jesus, now twelve years of age, going up to Jerusalem for the Passover. When the feast ended, his parents – thinking Jesus was in the caravan – did not seek him out until the day was past. After searching for him for three days, when they found him in the temple, his father said: "Son, how could you do this to us? Do you not realize we have been seeking you anxiously?" And Jesus replied: "How is it that you sought me? Do you not know that I must be in my Father's house?" Here is Christ declaring God to be his father, while his parents, standing before him, do not understand. If you are seeking the cause of the phenomena of your life among your kinsfolk, your acquaintances, or teachers, you will never find it; for you are God's temple, and the spirit of God dwells in you. The cause of the phenomena of your life is not on the outside, but in your own wonderful human imagination. Do you not realize that Jesus Christ is in you? I tell you, the only place you will ever find him is within!

The life of Jesus is a pattern which will unfold in you, an individual, when you discover yourself to be the cause of your life; for as He is, so are you in this world. Our religious leaders teach Christ as someone on the outside who is different; who overcame, and is now living elsewhere; yet Christ in you is your hope of glory, for as He is, you are!

---

[2] Isaiah 45

In his book, Luke tells the parable of Jesus, who – upon entering a boat with his disciples, falls asleep as they set sail. When a storm wind descended upon the lake they woke him, saying: "Master we are perishing." Then He rebuked the wind, and the raging waves became quiet, and there was a great calm. I tell you: the one who fell asleep caused the storm, and is the same being as the one who – upon awakening – quells it; for there is no other.

In this world Christ is asleep, and the wars, confusions, depressions, and horrors, appear because of his dreams. And the world will know no peace, happiness, wealth, or joy, until Christ awakes. If you are unaware of your imaginal activity, you are asleep relative to it. You could be dreaming noble, lovely dreams or ignoble ones; but whatever you dream, Christ will externalize. Man is the ark of God in which Christ – God's creative power – is contained. I am the ark of God, not a phantom of the earth and sea. I am the ship in which Christ sleeps as he dreams the storms of my life. And when He awakes, I will know calm and weal. Your own wonderful human imagination is Jesus Christ. Now individualized as John, Mary, Sam, or Sue, you are Christ's outer projection, surrounded by woes and weals because of his dreams. God, as your imagination, can never be so far off as even to be near, for the nearness implies separation. Wherever you are, I am! To say: "I am" is near, is to claim God is another – but there is no other. You and God are one, for He is your wonderful human imagination!

A friend recently shared this vision with me. As he observed buildings, trees, and houses round about him, he realized they were caused by tiny magnetic seeds which were clustered about his feet. As he scraped them off, they instantly reformed themselves to produce automatic changes in his world. What a wonderful experience! In the 40th Psalm we read: "He lifts me up from the pit, out of the miry bog and places my feet upon the Rock." Here we see the foot, the symbol of God's creative power, is lifted up and placed upon the Rock – the human imagination! His vision is showing him that he has now become aware of the only causation, and has placed his creative power upon that Rock. In this 40th Psalm the statement is made: "In the volume of the book it is written about me." My friend's vision reveals that he has come to that point. That everything which appears magnified on the outside is caused by magnetic seeds around his feet. This is true; for the world is nothing more than a magnified shadow, caused by the magnetic seed called Man. Although the world appears to be large and overpowering, its causation is the power observing it.

Man is the ark of God and everything is contained within him. Asleep, the storms rage; but when man awakes, the stormy seas will be no more.

There is quite a difference between being awake to your imaginal activities and being asleep to them. Awake, you can trace the event taking place on the outside to an imaginal act; but asleep you will find someone or something on the outside to be its cause. But causation is within the one observing the effect. Causation is symbolized as the foot in the 40th and 69th Psalms, as well as in the 10th chapter of Romans. In the end, man will overcome and put all things under his foot.

My friend saw the clusters of magnetic seeds around his feet. Although he tried to scrape them off, they reappeared. As Blake said: "The oak is cut down by the ax and the lamb is slain by the knife, but their forms eternal remain forever, returning by the seed of contemplative thought."

Our world is the storm spoken of in the 8th chapter of Luke. Having entered our body, we have fallen asleep to our creative power. But when we discipline our mind, we quell the storms. The disciples of scripture are disciplined aspects of the mind. Once your five senses are so disciplined you see, hear, taste, touch, and smell, only what you desire, then you quell the storms of doubt and fear within you, for you know who you are. No longer will you seek the phenomena of life among your kinsfolk or acquaintances; for when you awaken, you find life in the temple. The world is always looking for new teachers on the outside, when there is nothing there but shadows. Christ is not another. You are Christ, as he is your very self! You will find him, and when you do, you will know that you are God; for a series of events will unfold within you and you will bear witness to your own fatherhood.

I have often thought that the doctrine of the trinity should have been the doctrine of the being, for the trinity is difficult for man to grasp. It's easier to speak of the doctrine of revealed

Christianity as a unity, than as a trinity. When David stands before you as your son, there will be no more trinity. You and I are one when my son David calls you father! Then you will know that everyone in the world is that same being, as they will all have the same son. This is the great doctrine of the unity.

My old friend Ab always began his classes with the statement: "Praise be to that unity which is our unity." He knew that although we are a diversity of faces, completely individualized, we are the same father of God's one and only son, who will reveal himself to all, individually, thereby proving our unity of being.

Every scriptural miracle is an acted parable. It is imagination who enters the boat called man and falls asleep in order for the journey of life to begin. Then the financial, marital, physical storms arise according to man's dreams. He could dream of something lovely and know healthy, happy storms. But if he does not know that the cause of the weal is his imaginal activity, he will continue to dwell in the storms of life until the disciples rouse him to remembrance.

Awake, you are aware of the thoughts you are creating every moment of time, and carry this awareness into your dream world. You will not falter, for – knowing the world you want to build and its cause – you will be constantly aware of what you are imagining. You will no longer seek your desires among things, but will turn within to find they are all waiting to be fulfilled in God's temple.

Now, the numbers three and eight in scripture are always associated with resurrection. We are told that on the third day the earth rose up out of the deep, and in the Book of Exodus it is said that it came to pass on the eighth day. Luke tells us that when Jesus was twelve years of age, his parents searched three days before finding him in the temple, asking and answering his own questions. The number twelve is telling us that he had arrived at the point of creativity. That he has now resurrected and moved into the Father's house, for when they found him he said: "Why do you seek me? Do you not know I must be in my Father's house?" Having identified God as his Father, he goes on to claim: "I and my Father are one."

Today, as in that day, men cannot believe that imagination is the cause of the phenomena of life. They will agree that an artist can imagine a lovely picture and bring it forth on canvas, but they cannot relate the same technique to a toothache. Yet there is only one cause! I, the Lord, am the cause and there is no other. Besides me there is no God. I form light and create darkness. I make weal and create woe. I, the Lord, am he who does all these things. You cannot blame anyone for your misfortune. You could claim a friend betrayed your trust, therein causing your misfortune; but your friend was not the cause, your dream prompted you to confide in your friend. Causation is not on the outside, it comes from within. As you begin to awake, you discover there is only one God, who is your own wonderful human imagination.

My friend saw tiny, magnetic seeds swirling around his feet, causing the outer world to appear so large. These seeds of contemplative thought are so tiny they are often ignored and even scraped off; but awareness causes them to reform themselves instantly to magnify their new formation in the outer world. If imagination's seeds did not reform themselves, the outer world would vanish and leave not a trace behind; but they do, for the seeds are contained in man. You have the power to rearrange your thought-seeds to produce a different pattern in your outer world. This is done by a change of attitude. Think of the world as different, and as you do, you have scraped off the little magnetic seeds, thereby causing their rearrangement. This is the world in which we live.

Now, when imagination lifts us up from the pit and places our feet upon the Rock, we stand on our own feet. No longer will we stand upon the foot of another, giving the other either our praise or blame. We can, however, be gracious and kind and thank another for the role he played in our drama. But when we stand on our own feet, we realized that everything that happens – be it good, bad or indifferent – is because of our attitude towards life.

Every person, place, or thing, is animated and rearranged from within; for as He is, so are we. A good Christian would call that statement blasphemy; yet I am quoting the first epistle, the fourth chapter of the Book of John: "As he is, so are we in this world." This thought follows on the heels of the definition of God as love. And because God is love, He will not change your imaginal act, but will allow it to be externalized. If God changed the act, there would be two of you: one who imagines, and one who changes the imaginal act. But, being all love, God instantly plays the parts designated in your imaginal acts and suffers with you because He is dreaming. But one day Love will awaken within your skull. He will resurrect and you will begin the real drama, which is to discover your true identity. Coming out of your immortal skull, all of the imagery of scripture will surround you. The child and the witnesses will be there; but they will not see you, for you will be spirit. While witnessing your spiritual birth, they will speak of you and identify the child as yours, but you will be invisible to their mortal eye. As the great drama unfolds, it appears to take place externally; yet it is within, for you contain eternity within yourself.

If to you a storm is raging remember, it is only raging because you are not aware of your imaginal activity. By disciplining your thoughts, you rise from the sleep of unawareness, and become aware of what you want to imagine. Then the world will change to conform to the change in you. The storm will subside and there will be a perfect calm.

Do not look for God outside of the temple, for you are God's temple, and the spirit of God dwells in you. Ask the average person where he thinks God's temple is, and he will point to a synagogue, cathedral, or church; but God does not dwell in houses made with hands. God is spirit and dwells in his living temple! Imagine – and God is acting. Believe in the reality of what you are now imagining! Rearrange those little clusters around the foot, and when they are fixed with feeling, relax in the knowledge that your outer world will conform to the new fixation. Although the world appears external, its reality is within, as you are its creative power, dreaming the world into being; for you are an immortal being, wearing a garment of mortality. One day you will awaken from this fantastic dream, to find yourself enhanced by having experienced the mystery of death.

I ask you now to take the challenge and change your thinking, although I know it is not an easy thing to do. I have known those who so enjoy hating another that they do not want to change. They seem to receive a certain pleasure out of hating and do not realize that they are only hating themselves.

I remember a man in New York City during the Second World War, who claimed he despised Roosevelt. Every morning when the man shaved, he would talk to himself in the mirror, imagining he was telling Roosevelt everything he disliked about him. The gentleman attended my meetings, and when I confronted him with his imaginal acts, he said: "I pay $10 to see a Broadway show which does not give me the joy I receive during that ten minutes in the morning." Well, this man created his own storm, for the venom that he spewed out every morning returned to him. He lost his New York City home, then went to Florida, where he lost everything there. I tried to tell him to awake, that he was sleeping and only dreaming that Roosevelt was the cause of his world. But he could not believe me. He came from a Germanic background and could not get over the fact that we were at war with Germany. He blamed Roosevelt, even though he knew Germany had declared war on us. He could not see the war as a bad dream, and he was confusing it, making the storm rage by the pleasure he received telling Roosevelt off as he shaved.

It's entirely up to you what you think. If you want to hate someone, you can augment it through intensity and persistence. The same thing is true if you want to love someone; for your human imagination is the only God you will ever know, and he is in his temple – that temple you are!

The parents (meaning tradition) sought Jesus on the outside, but when they found him within, he said: "Do you not know that I must be in my Father's house?" but they could not understand. When I have told rabbis, preachers, and priests, that I have seen David of Biblical fame, they laugh. And when I go further and tell them that David called me father in fulfillment of the 89th Psalm which states: "I have found David, he has cried unto me, 'Thou art my Father, my God and Rock of my salvation.'" They stand silent, unable to make the Bible their biography.

As long as you think the Bible is speaking of someone other than yourself, you will never understand it. The entire book, from beginning to end, is all about you, individually. You are the one who will find David. It is you he will call "My Father, my God and the Rock of my salvation." David will literally stand before you as a young man just coming into adolescence. It is the same David who cried out in the Old Testament: "You will not leave me in the pit, in the miry bog." And you do not. You awaken and, after three days you find him in the temple and scripture is fulfilled.

I tell you: you are an immortal being whose autobiography is recorded in scripture. Having inspired the prophets of the Old Testament, you came into the world to fulfill their words in the New. As the universally diffused individuality, Christ is housed in every child born of woman, bringing him into the world by meditating him into being.

Take the story of my friend seriously. Think of your thoughts as magnetic seeds, invisible and miniature, and the world as bearing witness to their arrangement. And remember: all you need do is rearrange your power-filled thoughts, and you will produce a corresponding rearrangement in your outer world.

Now let us go into the silence.

CPSIA information can be obtained
at www.ICGtesting.com
Printed in the USA
LVHW041028060319
609682LV00003B/475/P